DROP THE MOTHERFUCKING STRUGGLE

DROP THE MOTHERFUCKING STRUGGLE

Your guide to creating an outrageously successful life by embracing your awesomeness

Susanne Grant

Drop The Motherfucking Struggle.

First edition August 2021.

For print, podcast or media interviews with Susanne, please contact love@reachsusanne.com.

Published by Grant Method Coaching and House of Hives.
Cover by Susanne Grant.
Photo by Hannah Grant.
Editing by Jonathan Campion.

ISBN Paperback: 978-1-5262-0888-0.

To my wonderful family.
I couldn't have done this without you.

YOUR FREE GIFT

Visit dropthestruggle.co.uk to receive free book resources to help you to drop the motherfucking struggle for good.

Access your resources here:
http://dropthestruggle.co.uk/

Contents

Praise

Drop the Motherfucking Struggle is a cheerful, unapologetic manifesto for anyone who is willing to leave the struggle behind, see what's available for them, and truly step into their worth. It's one of the best books I've read this year.

Silja Thor | Serial Entrepreneur & Business Mentor
siljathor.com

This book truly is like having a little Susanne in your pocket. Her no-nonsense approach to creating the life of your dreams jumps right off the page. This book gets you excited to sort your shit out and drop the motherfucking struggle for good.

Mags Thomson | Award-winning Editor-in-Chief
houseofhives.com

Drop the Motherfucking Struggle is the ultimate guide for women who have been taught that the hustle and grind is the only way to achieve success to discover how to take a step back and connect with themselves once again. Susanne Grant weaves in stories from her past, from clients, and important statistics to show that women (especially mums) truly have the power to take control and live the life of their dreams. Plus, the exercises and journal prompts provide the reader with incredible step-by-step support along the way. It's as though Susanne is right there with you, cheering you on.

Melanie Herschorn | Content Marketing Strategist
vipdigitalcontent.com

Introduction

I did not want to be a mother. After a very traumatic childhood, I believed this awful world was better off without me adding more to the pile. Until I received "the call" in 2012, I had never even considered finding myself a husband and settling down in the traditional sense. These conflicting feelings of what I desired growing up, and what society told me I was supposed to want, left me feeling torn. I was tired of struggling and thought many times of just throwing in the towel, if you catch my drift.

It wasn't until I met my husband, the father of my children, that all of these desires shifted. As soon as I became a mum, my dreams seemed to go out the window. Travelling the world and having an awesome kick-ass job doing some amazing things, like I used to dream about, felt impossible. I couldn't do it any more - or at least I felt like I wasn't supposed to. I felt stuck and very alone.

The success I was after, to begin with, was along the lines of: work hard, get a degree, get yourself a good job, then climb the corporate ladder until you get an even higher-paying job changing the world. The white picket fence, 1.7 children and a shiny trophy husband weren't part of the deal for me. And to be completely honest with you, I was told more than once to be an independent woman. Don't rely on anyone, especially not a man. So it was a big surprise to me that I found someone in this crazy world who managed to deal with my crazy shit.

By the time I reached my 30s, I was completely burned out. Life wasn't very fulfilling. At the time, I was in a relationship with someone I thought made sense. But I was miserable because deep down, I still believed that, no matter what I tried, I couldn't be happy. What was the point? Who was I to have that?

Things had to be hard to receive them, right? Because things were *never* easy. Everything was an uphill battle, and it seemed to get worse as the years progressed. The struggle was part of the deal. I had to struggle to be worthy of receiving anything. It was hard; life was hard. Especially being a mother on top of this later on. It was draining my life energy; making me feel tired, sad and frustrated.

On the night I turned 29, I had an epiphany. My mind received this huge download on how I was meant to serve the world with my gifts. This idea resulted in me starting my own business, a coaching company supporting women and their families which I called Grant Method Coaching.

A few months into my business I was introduced to mindset work by amazing and inspiring business owners. Thanks to them I started seeing all these - often unhelpful - patterns and beliefs in my own life playing out in front of me in the following years.

Things like:

- Get a good education and you will be successful
- Working hard equals success
- Work at least 60 to 80+ hours per week
- If you don't work enough, you just don't want it badly enough
- Everyone successful gets up at 5 am
- No pain, no gain

And many, many more...

I had to peel back the layers of who I thought I was, who I thought I was supposed to be, and uncover who I was meant to be, to create the success I deserved. And all whilst being a young mother in business.

This journey was a deep, raw and often lonely process. I had to look at myself and what I desired in life – and what I allowed and disallowed myself to have in the first place.

As a result of my traumatic upbringing, I believed I wasn't worthy of much. Well, that's not entirely true: to be completely honest with you I didn't think I was worthy of anything. Don't get your hopes up and always expect the worst. In the last few years my relationship with success has gone from hard work and struggle to ease, alignment and flow. But I made a lot of mistakes along the way, due to the trial and error of figuring this out all by myself.

In *Drop The Motherfucking Struggle - Your guide to creating an outrageously successful life by embracing your awesomeness*, you will learn how to shift your reality from struggle to ease, leaving the days of burnout, struggles and hardship in the past, as you allow yourself to be guided to create *your* version of outrageous success in a way that feels easy, fun and fantastic. You will be able to embrace a new way of doing and being.

Together we will uncover the truth about success; what it really means to be successful, how to create the success you desire, how to bring to life your personalised success strategy, and - most of all - how success feels to you, so you can create an outrageously successful life on your terms.

Even though this book is written with female business owners, CEOs and entrepreneurs in mind, you can still learn from it if you don't have a business (yet), as these principles can be applied in every area of your life. If you have opened this book and don't identify as female, please know you are just as welcome as anyone else in my world, but for ease of writing, I have used she/her pronouns. Feel free to substitute your preferred pronoun as you read. I am very glad you are here!

It is my pleasure and great honour to be guiding you through these pages, to show you how good life can become as we implement these new truths step-by-step into your life.

As with every journey, take as long as you need to fully understand my words, and let them resonate deeply within you. Allow them to give you the transformation you desire and deserve. You matter, and so do your dreams. We are not running a competition here, so take as long (or as little) as you need. In my universe there is no need to pretend you are something you are not.

You can decide to instantly claim your new life at this very moment, or do it more gradually. When it comes to your life, there is no right or wrong way of doing things; just make sure it feels good to you. But more on that later.

For now, are you ready to embrace your awesomeness to create an outrageously successful life on your terms?

Let's do this thing!

Xo, Susanne

The Truth About Success

"Know that there are ways to create your own rules and live in a different structure, in a different paradigm. Everyone would do it if they knew, but they don't know, don't believe and they refuse to fucking hear it."

Amanda Frances

It was the first few months after my baby girl was born. Those early days were intense, to say the least. I felt like I was chained to the earth with a heavy, handmade, forged metal chain hanging from my neck. Some days I could barely move, let alone breathe.

The chains held me down, forcing me to surrender to a force unknown to me at the time. It had a tight grip and it was suffocating me. Without realising, I had tapped into a deep, dark part of life; a part of history I was yet unfamiliar with, the collective suffering and suppression of all the women who had walked this earth before me. Was this the joyful experience of modern-day motherhood that society keeps telling us about?

From a young age, I have always been able to connect with my physical and spiritual body in a way many people don't understand. I can see things, hear things, and feel things about myself, other people and sometimes even worldly events. I receive pictures, mini-movies, sounds, words, but most of all guidance, like whispers in my right ear, about what to do or where I should go next.

I believe everyone is born with their own personal guidance system; their intuition. Our intuition is the connection to the higher self and guides us in navigating life in a way that is the most joyful and pleasant for us as a person. Unfortunately, along the way we often meet people who are convinced that *they* know what is right for us.

As we get older we stop listening to our own intuition, stop trusting our gut and our personal power. As a result, many of us are still trying to please a dead relative, or a parent or ex-partner, who isn't even around anymore. We do everything in our power to conform to what we think others, or society, expects us to do which is exhausting.

It usually goes something like this: go to school, get good grades, do as you are told, get a job, be a good girl, work nine-to-five for a steady paycheck, get married, buy a house, have children, retire, die...

But this old paradigm doesn't work for many of us anymore. I know many women who don't want children. I know couples who want an off-grid sustainable house and to retire at 40, or to travel the world with the family in a VW Campervan. Screw those old-fashioned social conventions! Yet often, when we decide to follow our bliss, we are made to feel bad for doing what makes us happy.

Growing up, I managed to piss off a lot of adults who were telling me to do something and my gut told me otherwise. I remember telling a teacher when I was eight, that it was nice for him to decide for me what I needed to do, but where was he going to be when I had to deal with the consequences of *his* decision? It was my life and if I was going to live it, the choices were going to be my own.

It threw people off when I spoke up and told them no and that was that. But more often than not, I was just dismissed as a rebel, a misbehaving girl. I was the bitch who didn't do as she was told when I refused to substitute my opinions for theirs.

Eventually, worn down, I tried to make myself fit the boxes, the judgements and perceptions placed on me. I had to be a good girl, to listen and to do what others expected of me. How else would people support me? At the same time, I was trying to listen to my intuition, and the guidance it was trying to give me. It was detrimental not only to my physical health but also to my mental health. It was like I was being pulled in several different directions.

Whatever I did, it was never good enough, because I could never please everyone. How can you trust yourself when everyone else tells you to do something different, claiming to know what's best for you?

During high school, it became the norm to study for 70 to 80 hours per week. Classes took up around 40 hours, and then there were homework assignments for every subject on top of that. There was no time to relax, let alone connect with yourself and let your intuition speak.

Every now and then some words or images fought their way through, but it became rarer as time passed. On top of that my health started to decline rapidly. I had always been prone to allergies and little niggles here and there, but it became much worse. I could barely eat due to stomach pains. I started to get neck and back pains. If I was lucky I would get three hours' sleep at night.

This always-busy pattern continued at university, where besides the 70 to 80 hours of academic work per week, I also had to keep a job to pay my way. On top of classes, assignments and work I had to do fieldwork as part of my course, so holidays went out of the window too.

Surprise, surprise, when my Master's degree came to an end, I was done. I was done working hard, I was done motivating myself to do things I didn't find that interesting to begin with. Even though I landed myself a high-paying corporate job as a data analyst right after university, I quickly realised that I needed a break.

Luckily, I was in a situation at the time where I could take time off, which was quite a shock on the system. For the first few weeks I felt petrified. The fear of doing nothing was something that rocked my system to its core.

Not having a schedule or homework; not knowing what I have to do 24 hours per day, seven days per week? It threw me off as I simply did not know what to do with myself. What did I enjoy doing that wasn't related to a goal, a programme, a subject, or someone making decisions for me? Who was I underneath all the busyness, endless to-do lists and goal-setting exercises?

Yet in these difficult times, I found the connection with myself again. When everything - all the shoulds and coulds - fell away, all there was left was me. Every thought, every emotion, every memory was put under a magnifying glass for me to re-examine.

As my life started to slow down and I connected with myself daily through meditation, I started to feel physically and mentally better. The back pains and stomach aches that I took for granted disappeared, and I slept a solid eight hours per night, at least.

My intuition was getting stronger and I was starting

to feel lighter. Life was fun again; things were flowing and I felt great pleasure in "just" being me.

Then one day, I received "the call".

A soul was calling me to become her mother. Initially, I was shocked because I never wanted to be a mother. I felt my childhood had been awful enough and I didn't want to bring a child into this world, especially with global events as they were. Besides, there are enough children who don't have parents, and I always dreamed of becoming an adoptive mum instead.

But this little soul was persistent; the little girl who we later named Regan became a daily visitor. She made it clear to me that I was her mother. However, my partner at the time was not going to be the father. I was confused. I had no intention of straying from the relationship or ending it. However, it became obvious that this wasn't the life that was meant for me.

Slowly my partner at that time and I started to grow apart. With my intuition growing day by day, I followed my gut to create this life. We didn't resonate as we used to, and we decided to separate in November that year.

At the end of December, I got a message from a friend who asked how I was doing. I chuckled as I saw the message and knew this little soul was guiding me to something. This friend and I met years ago and we had clicked, but because we lived in different countries things never really took off. For months we continued to talk, and we started to resonate on a deeper level.

As luck would have it, I got a financial windfall soon after and decided to book a ticket to visit my friends in the UK for a fun weekend away. My friend, my now-husband, and I got to spend time together this weekend too. As we sat next to each other, we were just quiet, not saying a word. When we tried to speak, words came out with great difficulty. It was like trying to move through mud.

However, our spirit teams were having a blast! It felt like they were having a party, celebrating finding each other, planning out the next steps in our lives together. They were all in. All we could do was sit there and enjoy the ride.

The weekend passed, and it was time to fly back. I barely managed to get myself on the plane, as every fibre of my being was telling me to stay.

When I landed at the airport, everything felt different. The colours, the smells, the sounds; this town - Amsterdam - that I loved so dearly, wasn't my home any more. It took me five weeks to tie up loose ends and move to beautiful Scotland that summer. It was such an easy and fun experience; whatever I needed, or wanted, all I had to do was ask, and it showed up.

Within weeks I had found a room to stay in and started this new chapter of my life. All the pieces were starting to fit together. My husband and I started dating and, after a while, we found out we were expecting baby Regan - the beautiful little soul that had been guiding me for almost a year. Until one afternoon I started to bleed.

I went to sleep and woke up a few hours later to discover my body had miscarried our beloved baby girl. I was in shock. I could not understand why she was part of my life for almost a year, guiding me towards every decision and opportunity, and then she left. She left! For weeks, even months, I cried, I screamed, I was absolutely devastated. Was this what my intuition was meant to bring me? All of this and then to lose her?

It took me a couple of years to be able to wrap my head around this experience. It had shaken me to my core. In the meantime, we got pregnant with another baby girl. Besides the - not so - morning sickness that lasted months and a relatively easy birth, thanks to the hypnobirthing course I did, the pregnancy was far less intense than the start of baby Regan's pregnancy. However, the journey into motherhood wasn't as smooth as I had hoped for.

Being alone in a new country, with no close friends or family to help, especially in the early days, was challenging. It felt suffocating. Limiting. Like I lost myself, and all I could do is be of service to this little baby, who depended on me for her life.

For the first six months in particular, when she could only breastfeed with me, I think - in hindsight - I was in a constant state of panic. What if I don't have enough milk? What if it isn't enough? What if I cannot do or be enough? It was doable - just. But I certainly didn't enjoy these first few months, and it wasn't until the first year had passed that I started to be able to truly bond with my beautiful baby.

When I became a mother for a second time a few years later, the busyness started to creep back in. Especially in those early stages, when it seems like you are feeding everyone around the clock and have zero time for yourself.

This time it was different, though. My little boy craved the quiet. He liked to just sit or snuggle when there were no other people or sounds around. Those quiet nights, the connection to myself, was still there.

Now that he is older, I need to make time for myself; to sit still and do nothing. There was always more laundry to do, or things to tidy up, but if I let that determine my schedule then my business would have gone on the back burner, never to be returned.

Somehow though now I am a mother, I don't know why, but suddenly I am expected to be responsible for everyone's dinner choices, present buying and social calendar organising. My husband's included. It's not like he is a grown-ass man who is more than capable of doing his own things...

I know so many women who are struggling with all the hats they have to wear; they are mums, partners, business owners or employees, sisters, daughters and more. The busyness becomes a badge of honour as we simply don't have time for the things that matter any more. If we are too busy to do what truly matters to us, does that mean we matter? That's where the paradox lies.

While often working for well over 80 hours per week, do you ever wonder why so many of us are struggling with our health and relationships? I believe this to be the real curse of modern-day womanhood; to be able to have it all only at the expense of our own wellbeing. Isn't it time for a new paradigm?

Are we secretly still appointing ourselves homework to avoid the stillness? Or as the singer Pink rightfully points out in her song Sober: *the quiet scares me 'cause it screams the truth*. Are we avoiding the quiet because we are afraid of our own truth?

Put your hand up if you grew up to be an independent woman? Be a good girl? Work hard? Get a degree and earn your way in life? Yes? I hear ya. It's the same crap I grew up with.

The problem with this is that we don't allow anyone to back us up, including our own emotional guidance system, other people, or the universe. Because no one can do it as well as we can.

If we don't work hard and we don't prove we are worthy, we do not receive the (financial) rewards of it. It leaves us stuck in an endless cycle of people-pleasing, whilst draining our spirit completely. Because, God forbid, life isn't meant to be easy, right?!

Have you ever woken up in the morning thinking about all the things that are going well for you and then, suddenly, the fear creeps in? Getting ready to brace yourself? Unconsciously, we often create an area in our life where we have to struggle.

If business is good, the marriage is suffering. If our health is good, business is slow. If the finances are great, our love life feels completely drained. Just to mention a few examples. Deep down most of us still believe we can't have it all.

It is culturally accepted that success has to come at a price. If you believe this to be the case, success *will* come at a price.

My story came with depression, gut health and period issues, as well as sleepless nights and strained relationships. I was told I wasn't good enough: the favourite catchphrase at home was, I was just "fat, stupid and ugly". It took me almost twenty years to break free of these untrue statements.

Growing up, it became pretty clear that other people didn't care about my opinion or how I felt. Being so strongly connected to my feelings and intuition in a world that was hard and feeling disconnected was tough.

The most confusing thing was that most adults around me seemed to have no clue about what was the right way to go. One adult would say one thing, one would say another, but they never seemed to agree and they would argue a lot because of it.

Somehow, somewhere, we lost the connection to ourselves, and the inner voice that whispers (or shouts if you don't listen) to help you to find your way in life. It is an endless cycle of trying to please people and make them happy, even if these people have no clue themselves about how to make them happy. Add on top of that our addiction to staying busy and our fear of missing out, and it is no wonder that so many of us are struggling our way through life.

What if being (too) busy comes at a price, costing you your health and your relationships? Is that a price that we should be willing to pay, as an individual or as a society? The healthcare costs of job-related burnout are currently guesstimated between $125-$190 billion per year.[1] Not to mention many stress-related illnesses that could be completely prevented, if we would address this "work hard until you drop" paradigm as a culture properly.

Many entrepreneurial gurus believe that "working hard" and "hustle" is the only way to be successful. If you don't put in 80 hours, you just don't want it badly enough. If you are currently trying to grow your business and create the success you want, I am sure you've seen many of these - false - messages on how to be successful by using this one particular strategy. Do you find yourself buying endless online courses promising you *the* answer?

The worst and most harmful business strategy is the advice to "work hard and it will pay off". And to be honest, this is awful advice not just for business,

---

[1] Marnie Dobson Zimmerman, PhD & Peter Schnall, MD MPH, *The Cost of Burnout: Why We Need Healthy Work*, Healthy Work Now. Accessed 11 Jul. 2021, https://healthyworknow.medium.com/the-cost-of-burnout-why-we-need-healthy-work-8a552a151603

but for life in general. This advice, and the whole hustle-until-you-drop culture, is very detrimental to your (mental) health. So what if there is another way to be deeply wealthy - in all areas of your life, and not just your bank account? What if you can have it all and live a rich and fulfilling life?

There is nothing wrong with working hard and enjoying what you do. However, "work hard" is not a solid business strategy on its own. If you are working on the wrong thing for 80 percent of your time, of course, you will notice the progress you make, but you will probably also feel very tired and drained.

I tried for many years to do as much as I could. Those 60 to 80+ hours per week left me completely burned out in the end.

So yes, work for your dreams - but work on the things that are actually useful for your goals, and incorporate rest in your strategy too. Because you *cannot* run a business successfully when you are on the verge of a breakdown.

That's why the hustle culture is so incredibly harmful. It paints a picture where destroying your own (mental) wellbeing is part of what it means to be successful. If this was really true, that hard work equals the most success and income, then nurses, teachers and waiters would be the ones making the most money of us all.

It made me wonder. What is missing from this equation? What are we not being told about success and creating the life we desire? What is missing from this picture?

The Lies We've Been Told

"We need to accept that we don't always make the right decisions, that we'll screw up royally sometimes. Understand that failure is not the opposite of success, it's part of the success."

Arianna Huffington

Success looks different to every person. When I was growing up, success was defined as getting a good degree and a nine-to-five job, until you retire and you can begin to enjoy life. In my family, I was taught that success was getting excellent grades (without praise). Later on, it was also the number in the bank account, and looks - well, mostly how much I weighed - that mattered most.

Luckily, I loved exploring new things, and I had a knack for numbers and history. However, the picture of the white picket fence, 1.7 children, a financially secure husband and a steady job didn't resonate with me at all.

I wanted to travel and experience freedom. Learn languages, dive into different cultures, and experience their way of being. That's personally still one of the things I love most: how amazing and fascinating (and sometimes really painful and traumatic) the history is of all these different people around the world. I love connecting with others in this way, it is what makes my heart sing.

In your family or culture, there may have been various standards and stories about success. Was it just available to white rich men? Did you have to become a total tight-ass bitch to get to the top? Was it something you could relate to and did it feel possible for you? Or was it only through a lot of sacrifices and extremely hard work that you could have just a fraction of success? Take a few moments to think about how your family and the culture you grew up in defined success before you continue. We will journal on this later.

For anyone who grew up between the 1950s and 1970s in main Europe, this "hard work mindset" seemed to be the consensus. Especially if the countries they grew up in were directly involved in the Second World War. After the war, it was time to work hard, rebuild the country and its economy, and get yourself a good stable job with a great employer for the rest of your life. You would buy a house and then sell it later for a big profit to enjoy your retirement, or live there mortgage-free.

Unfortunately, over the past decade or so, we have seen the property market crash, leaving a lot of people in huge amounts of debt and unable to make payments on their houses. In the area where I live, you need to pay a percentage in cash to get a mortgage, which means for the average family home this is a cash investment of £50,000 or more.

Most of us, in average jobs or as small business owners, don't have that kind of money lying around. The "work hard and you will have a secure future" lie we were told by older generations just doesn't apply to the current situation. Yet many of us still get pushed in that direction because "that's the thing to do".

Now, don't get me wrong - there is a lot to be said for having a great foundation that comes with getting an education and job. But it is not the *only* way to be successful in life.[2]

If more money and a degree is the goal, you can find yourself on a never-ending journey to chase

---

[2] Yes, with certain jobs it's a must, I agree.

more money and more degrees. And even though degrees and plenty of money can give you certain means in life, there is more to the equation which we are not being told.

What I've discovered - and what I've experienced with my clients as well - is that no amount of success is going to fix the fact that you feel incomplete or unworthy on the inside. No number in your bank account is going to fix your problems (although it can give you opportunities for sure). Some of my clients make seven-plus figures and are deeply unhappy with their current life, desperate for a change.

If you look up the meaning of the word success, you will get different definitions.

Success:

- Degree or measure of succeeding
- The favourable or desired outcome also: the attainment of wealth, favour, or eminence.
- One that succeeds
- Obsolete: outcome, result [3]

---

[3] "*Success.*" Merriam-Webster.com Dictionary, Merriam-Webster, Accessed 11 July 2021, https://www.merriam-webster.com/dictionary/success

As you can see, the meaning of success is rather broad. One definition says it is about achieving goals and the desired outcome by society's standards such as wealth. But you can also see it is a measure of a certain level of success. Which begs the questions: who sets these standards? Who gets to decide what makes you successful? What makes us successful to begin with?

Many of us are trapped by the people-pleasing standard of success. What makes you successful in *their* eyes? What should you be doing according to *them*? Will *they* accept you if you achieve X success? This pattern of trying to please others will drive you crazy, and will keep you in a place where - no matter what you do - it will *never* be enough. You will never feel like you are enough. Can you relate?

Let me paint you a picture. Growing up, I was a strong, tall, beautiful and intelligent brown-eyed girl. I believed I could achieve anything I set my mind to and worked hard to get there. Often I was called a bitch (for knowing what I wanted and not allowing them to forcefully bend me to their wills), which to me was only a compliment. But on the inside, I felt cold, cut off and disconnected. My depression started at the early age of six, and I started planning my suicide around eleven. I attempted this a few times in the years to follow.

I was raised to be an independent woman: be strong, be powerful, and don't rely on anyone. Especially not a man! A man is not a plan. The whole "I don't need anyone" vibe left me unable to deeply connect to myself and others, because I thought I was better off doing things alone and my way.

To this day, I still struggle with letting people help, like my husband hanging up or folding the laundry, as it is incredibly triggering when things aren't done "the right way" (aka my way). Because of this pattern, I've kept everyone - and everything - outside of me for the longest time. I don't need any help; I can do this alone, and I will. This left me completely, utterly miserable and completely burned out.

We are told to do it all by ourselves. And if we fail, because we can't work 100 hours per week, run our business and still do family life on top of that, we are failures because we should just try harder, not complain and be a bitch about it. The way we are raised, especially as part of the whole "independent superwoman" syndrome, is a sure way to make you fail. It will keep you stuck in the too-busy-not-enough-time cycle of constantly chasing up things, because there is simply too much to do by yourself. Success doesn't have to look like this.

Modern-day motherhood is an impossible task that we are "supposed" to carry out by ourselves, with as little help as possible. And if we do ask for help we should be ashamed about it. It is clear that in regard to equal rights, access to education, safe pregnancy, childbirth and support with raising a family, the system is falling short. Unless we are willing to stand up for ourselves, and other women, we will fail. It is simply too much for one person to do. If you are struggling with this, join the club: we have jackets.

The invisible work that is required to manage a household is often referred to as *emotional labour*. It's the mental load of always having to remember things that have to be done. Whether it is another pile of laundry, or dentist appointments or date night, this invisible workload is what is keeping you exhausted most days.

Always having to remember something, having to do something, never being able to switch off, is what is hurting you the most. Again, this is one of these lies we are told - that women are better at multitasking. The fact is, it has nothing to do with gender, and everything to do with what we've seen before, and how the more you do something, the better you get at it.

You are not solely responsible for everyone in the family unit, although it can certainly feel this way. As I mentioned before, I became responsible for all the appointments for my (ex) partners, and if I didn't organise it, I was told that I was sabotaging their friendships or relationships. Never had it crossed their minds that I simply had nothing to do with it. I believed - and still do - that if a friend of mine or my partner wants to meet someone, they can arrange it themselves. It is not up to me to plan any dentist or doctor's appointments, grandmother visits or make sure the washing is done. Does this sound familiar?

But somehow through years of social and cultural conditioning, this is what is expected of women and I for one, am not willing to play that game anymore. Because the price of these lies is high. I don't know about you, but I know I've kept myself small for way too long. I didn't think I was worthy of anything, let alone everything. It was a constant struggle to get things done, to achieve what I wanted.

Now, I am not one to shy away from hard work, so I did. I worked hard, just to prove that I could do it. I was worthy. I was good enough. But only when I achieved these goals and I got to do these things I desired.

Not believing in your own awesomeness is costing you more than you realise. Your ability to create a life you desire can have different effects in different areas of your life. Healthwise this can show up in different kinds of ways.

For me, this came mostly at the expense of my mental health. I was diagnosed with Post Traumatic Stress Disorder (PTSD) after I left home at seventeen. It took me years to find my way. I remember feeling incredibly lost in this big world, on my own and completely unprepared. The first few years were absolutely horrible and it took a long time to climb my way out of it.

Luckily, with the help of an amazing GP in Amsterdam, I was able to break this cycle. Together, we created a new plan going forward and, as they say, the rest is history.

This time of my life was definitely one of the lowest. I wasn't able to eat, sleep or get out of bed. It all tied in with the belief that I wasn't worthy. I had to suffer (why else would people treat me that badly?) and most of all, I had to do it all alone. Those three beliefs combined are a recipe for total disaster. It wasn't until I hit rock bottom that I managed to climb out, because the only choices I had left were to die or to figure this out.

As you can imagine, the relationships I had at that time weren't a great success either. I manifested more drama through them, or I just couldn't cope with the constant PTSD and anxiety attacks. In other words, the lie about not being able to have it all sabotaged many relationships, including my one with myself.

Think about this for a second. What do you believe about relationships? Are they easy? Are they fun? Are they abusive (been there)? Do they lift your spirit? Or do they feel draining and soul-sucking? What do you believe about how relationships should be? Can you have it all?

The fascinating thing is that when we believe we can't have it all, or have to suffer and struggle to be worthy enough, it is like living your life permanently with a blindfold and ear muffs on.

They may look cute and make you feel like you are wearing a badge of honour - "look at me suffering here" - but long-term it will drain your soul. Because you keep yourself closed off from people, opportunities and all the yummy goodness this world has to offer. And consequently, you will miss out on the things that *really* matter to you.

No matter what level of success you achieve, the number of goals you hit, or the sacrifices you make, you will never be truly successful if you don't *feel* successful. Real success is a powerful state of being, a feeling within, that allows you to stand in your power and shine your light in this world.

However, the struggle is optional. You get to decide if you want to keep playing the game that includes hardship, hard work, struggle, endless hours, painful periods and back pains and sleepless nights.[4] We create our reality, and these lies and limitations we've been sold are only required if we

---

[4] Obviously, there are some medical exceptions here, but a lot can be resolved through preventative medicine with the right tools and support

believe that they are an essential part of our life. But more on that in the next chapter.

Journaling questions:

As we are diving into uncovering what lies you have been told about success, I would love to invite you to do some journaling on this. You can use some pen and paper, or purchase the *Drop The Motherfucking Struggle Journals* I've created just for you. You can get yours under "Journals" at http://dropthestruggle.co.uk/.

Please answer the following questions before continuing to the next chapter:

- What lies have you been told about success?

- How were you supposed to be or act?

- Did you have to work hard to be successful?

- Did success come at a price? If yes, what was the price you had to pay?

There Is No Limit

"Whether you think you can or you can't, you're right."

Henry Ford

We live in a world that's made out of energy. Everything around you, including yourself, comes from the same source. Only a small percentage of this world is made out of matter. Matter is anything that has mass and volume, so in other words anything that takes up space. This includes you and the book you are holding, for example.[5] Only 0.0000000000000000000042 percent of the universe contains matter.[6] So in other words, almost everything is energy.

---

[5] TechTarget Contributor, *Matter*, WhatIs.com. Accessed 11 July 2021, https://whatis.techtarget.com/definition/matter
[6] *If you were to move all of the matter in the universe into one corner, how much space would it take up?* 1 April 2000, HowStuffWorks.com. Accessed 11 July 2021, https://science.howstuffworks.com/dictionary/astronomy-terms/question221.htm

We've been told our world is limited. There is only so much money, so much space and so many opportunities available. Therefore we'd better fight for what we want in life, otherwise someone else might steal our slice of the pie. However, this limiting belief comes from a place of scarcity, and it can keep you stuck for many years, if not for the rest of your life.

The truth is, you are so much more than just flesh and bone. And because this world is made up of energy, you and I are connected. Look around you and see what is in your room. The empty space, the air, all of it is actually energy. Because everything is energy, everything is connected, like an invisible web that is cast all over this universe. This means your thoughts allow you to connect to others, and vice versa.

Have you ever had the experience of thinking about a friend who just happens to call you seconds after? You may think this is a coincidence but there is no such thing. Everything is connected through this energetic web. This means you are also connected to your dreams and desires by using the power of your thoughts, even if they aren't here - yet.

This world is brilliantly designed to help you make your wildest dreams come true. Yes, even if you were dealt a shitty hand of cards (been there, my friend). There are all kinds of different laws that are here to support and guide you, such as the law of gravity and the law of attraction, to name just two. The law of gravity comes in handy when you are trying to move around and not drift off into space. The law of attraction is here to support you to create more with the thoughts and feelings you send out, because it is designed to match your frequency. Hence its name, the law of *attraction*. It will always give you more of the (un)wanted depending on your frequency.

When creating an outrageously successful life and business by embracing your awesomeness it is important to understand how this world works from an energetic point of view. The universe isn't testing you or making you work hard enough, so when you are ready you finally get to receive what you desire. God isn't punishing you or holding you separate from what you desire.

We see the world around us the way we think it is supposed to look. You get to decide how the world shows itself to you. This universe has an unlimited amount of options available for you, and because of the different laws all supporting you, it will rearrange itself in a way to align itself with what you believe. This whole universe revolves around you. Yes, it really does!

Knowing that you get to decide how the universe rearranges itself to match your beliefs, gives you very important insider knowledge on how to be successful in life. Looking at your current life, it is time to take stock and see where you are currently at. This is what I like to call your energetic set point. This will be your starting point moving forward.

The biggest question you can ask yourself is: what do you accept for your reality to be true? For me, I used to think I had to work at least 60 to 80 hours a week to pay the bills. As it turned out, there was also a reality available where ten hours, plus some passive income, was a way to pay the bills and then some.

I grew up in a household where it was made clear, over and over again, that I was unwanted and a nuisance to all. I had to adjust to everyone's needs, ignore my own, and make sure everyone (except for me) was ok. Any health issues that they experienced were caused by me, and I was responsible for fixing them. As you can imagine, it was an impossible task for a child to fulfil.

I am sure you can relate to the child - grown up paradigm to some degree, if not completely. You listen to your parents and you respect authority. Don't talk back and do as you are told. Any other behaviour is seen as misbehaving and us girls better know "our place".

When I left home at seventeen I found myself homeless for about nine months (luckily I could spend my nights staying with different family members and friends), but I clearly remember what a shock to my system this was. I realised that not everyone is trying to manipulate you, hit you, abuse you or control you. Yet I was constantly preparing myself for the worst-case scenario - which coincidentally I always made happen, thanks to the effectiveness of the law of attraction.

What I noticed was that the more I focused on these negatives, the more I created these situations for myself. And it made me wonder: what if I am the one who is creating these scenarios?

Slowly, I started to shift these negative rants inside my head by focusing on more positive things, or just by keeping my mind busy with things like music, cleaning or hanging out with friends. As I had these negative thoughts less and less, I also noticed - of course - that fewer of these worst-case scenarios were happening. I remember thinking that if I do have some control over what is created in my life, what is it that I do want to create? And step by step I started implementing these changes in my life.

It made myself no longer available for certain things in my life, like shitty boyfriends who abuse you or cheat on you. Or jobs that suck the life out of you because they don't align with your core desires. These changes didn't happen overnight, but gradually, one by one, things were starting to fall into place. I realised that I was the one in control of my ability to create.

This world is created so you can go out there and create a life worth living. The biggest shift you can choose to make, and I hope my words will inspire you to do so, is that you know and feel that you are worthy of making all your dreams come true. You don't need to prove anything; you don't need to change anything about the way you look or the number when you stand on the scales. You are enough, you are good enough and you always will be good enough. No matter how much or how little you decide to do.

Realising you can have it all and create a life on your terms is huge. Because we live in a vibrational universe, and with most of this world being energy - and not matter - you get to think things into existence. You are worthy of anything you want to be, do or have. And you get to decide what that is.

Think about it. Everything you see around you, was someone's thought, someone's dream or vision to create. Everything around you is *proof* that dreams do come true. You get to decide this for yourself. No one is forcing you to take back control, but the power to focus your thoughts to create is your birthright. You have free will, which allows you to make your life as good or as miserable as you want it to be. You get to decide that you want to feel good about who you are, right here, right now.

There is a lot of noise telling you that you need to be something different. Advertisements telling us to lose weight, bounce back after the baby, and behave like some kind of cartoon character in a comic who can bend out of shape just to please everyone - except ourselves. How do you get to know the real you underneath all the years of conditioning and people-pleasing? I will help you uncover your personal patterns later on, but now let's dive into how your life is keeping you stuck exactly where you are.

Please take the time to answer and reflect on these journaling questions. I recommend you get one of the journals that I've created just for you on the website https://dropthestruggle.co.uk/. You can also use a piece of paper or your phone. Writing away these perceived limitations, which you can then throw away (or burn those motherfuckers!) can be very therapeutic. But do what feels right for you.

Journaling questions:

- What do I have to accept in order for my current reality to be true?

- Do I limit myself by believing this? If yes, in what areas of my life do I keep myself stuck?

- What if there truly is no limit? What would I like to do with my life?

- If I am always supported (financially) and I am free to do what I want, what would I like to be, do and have?

Now, us humans have the funny habit of trying to make things as complex as possible. Especially around this topic where we dive into the energetics behind this, it is easy to start overthinking. This concept of *there is no limit* is true from a vibrational point of view.

You get to decide what kind of limits you place on yourself and your surroundings and in the next few chapters I will give you the practical know-how, allowing you to officially drop the motherfucking struggle and replace it with ease, fun and flow.

But for this to work for you, you have to decide that there is no limit. You are unlimited. Your options are unlimited. And you *can* create the life you want. Maybe you don't know all the answers yet. Maybe you don't know how. But you have the power. You had the power all along, even though many people have tried to convince you otherwise.

You are powerful beyond measure and you get to decide what you want to create. You are here on earth because you are a creator. Your energy, your body is made out of the same stuff that created this whole damn universe. That's how powerful you are. And you get to decide - right here, right now - that you are worthy of making your wildest dreams come true. How? I will explain this in the next few chapters.

Are you ready?

Cutting Through The Daily Bullshit

"'Crazy-busy' is a great armor, it's a great way for numbing. What a lot of us do is that we stay so busy, and so out in front of our life, that the truth of how we're feeling and what we really need can't catch up with us."

Brené Brown

Many of us are trapped in the "too busy" cycle; the hustle, the grind, "non-stop until you drop" mentality. Working with self-proclaimed busy bees and workaholics whose mental health, physical wellbeing and relationships are affected by their work ethics, has given me great insight into the stories we tell ourselves and the myth about what being too busy really means. Because it will come as no surprise to learn that being too busy actually has a deeper meaning. Let's find out what that meaning is...

In our society, being busy is often seen as a badge of honour. The hustle is widely promoted as a valid strategy for success. In addition, it is culturally widely accepted that being too busy is a valid excuse not to show up or be present at all.

We all know that being chronically too busy can lead to too much stress, which will affect our health and relationships. Medical research estimates that as much as 90 percent of illness and disease is stress-related.[7] So why do we choose this way of being, if we know it is harmful? Even when there are easy ways to resolve this destructive and harmful pattern?

There are several reasons why you can keep yourself stuck, even when you know the benefits of treating time differently. Years, if not generations, of conditioning come into play here. If you have been "fighting" to break this pattern, don't worry about it, you are not the first person stuck in this pattern and you won't be the last.

To get a better understanding of these deep-rooted patterns it is important to understand where they come from. Because when you know where you

---

[7] Clemson University Cooperative Extension Service, *Stress Management for the Health of It*, National Ag Safety Database, Accessed 11 July 2021, https://nasdonline.org/1445/d001245/stress-management-for-the-health-of-it.html

are, you know where you can go. These are the four most common reasons why you keep yourself under the busy spell.

Fear Of Missing Out

If you are always running around, saying yes to too many things and feeling flustered as more things land on your desk... You *will miss out* on the important things. That is just a fact. You will forget yet another birthday or anniversary. That meeting with that investor you were supposed to organise. Or the school play you *promised* you would make it to this time.

Yet the *Fear Of Missing Out* (FOMO), is real for many of us, perhaps even for you. This is often the biggest trap you can find yourself in. FOMO is causing you to miss out on things that truly matter to you, such as quality time with yourself, loved ones or aligned opportunities. And, more importantly, a deeper connection with life itself; a sense of fulfilment and the expression of your soul path.

FOMO is rooted in trust and safety. It means that if you trusted yourself, others and the universe to deliver what you desire and trusted yourself to take action when opportunity knocks, you would not be running around jumping on every opportunity, *hoping* that this is the thing that will make you feel X (just fill in yours: complete, free, safe, loved, etc).

You can completely resolve this pattern by learning to listen carefully to your body and intuition. But to be able to tune in like this, you need to stop being so freaking busy all the time. For most women, this is currently a never-ending cycle of frantic running around, trying to jump on the next thing and the next thing and the next thing, scared you are missing out on the good stuff you are desperately looking for. This brings me to point number two.

You are overwhelmed

We live in an era where there is an abundance of options available to us. But because there is so much choice, it is, in fact, hard to make a choice. The information overload from different platforms, such as social media and advertising, or even the many options of hummus and olives at your local shop, will be even further amplified if you are experiencing a real fear of missing out, as I mentioned above.

The combination of these two can create a lot of inner turmoil, which I call a "system overload". Too much choice will lead to you feeling overwhelmed some - if not all - of the time.

Overwhelm may show itself in different ways in your life. It may feel like your head is about to explode because of all the things that are going on. You may lie awake at night thinking. Or you feel tired all the time, just scrolling away on Facebook brainlessly for hours.

If this is you, again, this is a very normal experience in our modern-day life. It can become completely paralysing, resulting in you not even wanting to get out of bed some days.

This feeling ties in with years of conditioning around having to be the good girl, behave, follow in line and do as you are told. Over the years, we get taught not to listen to our bodies and our inner voice, and as a result, most of us feel completely lost by the time we are adults. The solution? It is time to connect back to yourself, and allow you to be ok with you.

You don't have a clear goal, sense of direction or purpose

If you don't know where you are going, it doesn't matter what road you take. Read that again. When you are too busy and overwhelmed, it doesn't matter what you do. You can get up, do your things and the law of attraction will still do its best to deliver what you want. But the results are sporadic at best. If you want to take back the control you can have over your life, then making time for what matters to you, making time for you, is essential.

To beat your busy pattern for good and move away from overwhelm, it is vital you have clarity about what matters to *you* and the life *you* want to create. So, think about all the different areas of your life, financially, emotionally, spiritually, physically and mentally speaking. What do you want to create in each area of your life?

If your choices do not align with the goals you are working towards (for example, you want to become fit again, but you keep watching Netflix and eating cake every evening), you have to leave these decisions in the past and start moving that cute ass of yours now. In other words, *learn to say no* if it doesn't serve the goal you are working towards.

Time and time again, I see the same issue with my clients. They don't have a clear vision or goals in mind, so they don't know what to do next. Hence the overwhelm.

If you don't know what the goal is, it doesn't matter what path you take. This means you keep being too busy as you are working on the wrong things, with little or no results. This is why you are not managing to move forward on the things that matter to you. This brings me to the final reason why you are stuck in your busy life.

You don't have clear boundaries

Because you don't have clarity, because of the information overload, you are not spending your time effectively. For example, saying yes when you want to say no, giving too much of yourself when your body tells you that you should rest. Or not communicating your needs to those around you in a constructive manner (so you can be deeply supported).

All of this will lead to adding to the "too busy" pile because you are simply doing too much or too many things you don't want to be doing. And let's face it, that is bloody exhausting.

If you want to kick the busyness to the curb, you need to create time to clarify what you need to do next. And that's the crux of the story, isn't it? You've got to make time to sort out the overwhelm when you are already too busy. And then to figure out what you need to be doing next instead is an almost impossible task.

Becoming aware of your chronic, too busy pattern may be a painful and confronting experience. We are so used to it being an acceptable way of functioning in life. I've been there and I have seen the impact that stress, anxiety, and overwhelm can have on our health, both physical and mental, and relationships. But just like your money mindset or business mindset, your time mindset - in other words, how you relate and interact with time - is important.

Exercise & Journaling Questions

If you want to start to take back control over your life and what you are aligning yourself with, I'd like you to start with a simple exercise that allows you to create awareness around what your patterns are.

If you know where you are at, you know what you are working with.

I recommend you use the free download I've created for this exercise to track your activities, so you can fully benefit from the power of shifting these patterns. You can find it with the other resources at http://dropthestruggle.co.uk/

Step number 1 - Tracking

To know where you are at, you need to start tracking your activities. It doesn't need to be complicated at all, so use the form I've created, or use your phone. Or even just use some paper.

You want to start gaining awareness of what is in your life and why you say yes to certain things. Do this exercise for at least a few days, or a week if that feels right, to get the insight we need from this exercise.

What I need you to do is time your activities this week. How long does it take to do everything you do? This includes work, your commute, getting the kids ready, any household chores and sleep. Every week has 168 hours, of which we only spend about

56 on sleep (8x7). So what are you spending the other 105 hours per week on? Let's find out by tracking your daily activities.

Step number 2 - Reflecting

After this week, I need you to look at the different elements in your life, and the things you are saying yes to.

- The five activities that took up most of my time were (for example sleep, work, travel and prepping meals):

- Did I say yes to things I want to do most of the time (for example school activities for the kids)?

- Did I spend a lot of time "mindlessly" scrolling on my phone or watching TV? If yes, what seems to be the trigger or pattern?

- Did I spend time on things I desire to do (for example reading, painting, crafting, learning a new skill) and if yes, for how long?

Step number 3 - Journaling

After you are done with these tracking exercises, do some journaling on the following questions:

- What do I want to create in each area of my life? Break it down: what do I want to achieve financially / emotionally / spiritually / physically / mentally?

- How do I feel about not making the progress I want?

- What recurring thoughts am I having?

- Why am I telling myself that these thoughts are true (ie. I am not good enough, I am wasting time, I will never achieve X goal)

- Is this ultimately true? Hint - if it feels bad, it never is

- What could be truer?

If you want to use the special journals I've designed for this book, you can purchase yours on Amazon via the http://dropthestruggle.co.uk/ website.

TRACKING

ACTIVITY	MONDAY	TUESDAY	WEDNESDAY	THURSDAY	FRIDAY

DROP THE MOTHERFUCKING STRUGGLE TRACKING EXERCISES

Achieving Your Wildest Dreams

"The way to get started is to quit talking and begin doing."

Walt Disney

Are you ready to make your wildest dreams come true? Then this is the chapter you have been waiting for! As tempting as it may be, I encourage you to read the other chapters first before starting with this one. The previous chapters help us to set some solid foundations together, allowing you to embrace your awesomeness once and for all, so you can achieve your wildest dreams and drop the struggle for good. Yay!

As you know, I have created several resources to go with this book, which you can download for free at http://dropthestruggle.co.uk/. There you can benefit from several powerful resources, including a guided meditation.

This guided meditation helps you to create your new life from *your vision* of the future instead of the memories of the past allowing you to open yourself up to all the yummy goodness this world has to offer you.

I recommend listening to the meditation at least once a day, preferably before bedtime. I purposefully used gentle and heartwarming music, so you can get yourself a good night's sleep with the new vibes doing their magic in your energy field, and you can fall asleep with a smile on your face.

If you need a pick-me-up during the day, or prefer to start your day with some upbeat happy music, my feel-good playlist is perfect for you to use. It will help you start your day fully aligned and energised. Use it as much as you want to shake your booty and get your energetic creation juices flowing. Remember we are creating a life of abundance. A bun dance! Get your body moving.

To access all the free resources please visit http://dropthestruggle.co.uk/. All you have to do is put in your details and they are all yours.

It's time to start thinking about what you want to create during and after reading this book. In the previous chapters we started to create awareness around where you are and where you would like to go, as well as the energetics behind creating better alignment for you to achieve your goals easily.

I am sure you picked up this book because you are done with the motherfucking struggle and everything that comes with it. Because let's face it, life is too short to be miserable. But before we start creating more clarity for you around this, it is important to point out that these negative experiences and thoughts aren't all bad. Let me explain.

Introduced in the early 1980s by John Welwood, a Buddhist teacher and psychotherapist, the term *spiritual bypassing* must be part of the conversation if we want to get the full benefit from this book.

The harmful practice of bypassing is extremely unhelpful when trying to create your dream life, and must be addressed before we continue. So what is bypassing? Spiritual bypassing is a tendency to use spiritual ideas and practices to sidestep or avoid facing unresolved emotional issues, psychological wounds, and unfinished developmental tasks.

Saying things like:

- Everything happens for a reason
- Good vibes only
- Stop being so negative

You may be bypassing without knowing it. Your feelings are a powerful, strong and helpful tool that can either support you or keep you where you are. If you are struggling with your mental health, such as with depression and anxiety, like I did for many years, being told to "just get over it" isn't helpful at all. And by the way, you don't get over things, you get through them.

What I have found helpful over the years is a technique shared by Abraham-Hicks Publications. They explain how you can shift negative emotions towards a more positive feeling by going general. You can't go from being depressed to extremely happy. The vibrational gap is too big and you just can't get there like that. But what you can do is make small shifts, make gradual changes, and as you keep shifting day by day, it will all add up in the end.

Negative feelings and experiences are a powerful way to show you what you want in life, because the moment you realise something is happening that you don't want, the desire of what you do want is also born. Later in this chapter I will show you exactly how to do this.

So if you know what you don't want, you know what you *do* want. And I am here to help you figure this out; to help you connect with your deepest desires.

Being honest about what you truly want can be scary as fuck. It can bring up all kinds of triggers. Now, of course, I don't want to scare the bejeebers out of you before we even get started, but I do want you to be aware that there can be many triggers that can surface. But don't worry - it's nothing we can't deal with together.

It's not uncommon for our safety trigger to become active. For example, you may want to travel the world by yourself for the next year, but you are afraid to lose your partner. Or you want to sell your current business and start a completely new one selling handmade socks. I don't know why I am thinking about my socks right now, but let's roll with it.

Giving up what you know for something new can feel pretty darn scary. But the thing is, our bodies are designed to work this way. Where we are is safe (unless you are in an unsafe environment right now, in which case, I urge you to leave or call for help if possible), because we are familiar with the environment.

Moving towards something new or unknown also means that we don't know if our bodies will be safe there too. This mechanism has been around for as long as humans have been walking this earth. And it has done a good job protecting us, as there are over eight billion of us on the planet right now.

However, this same principle can hold you back or keep you stuck. It can create an endless cycle of wanting to move forward, only for you to chicken out because of this in-built safety mechanism that is millions of years old. It may have been handy for avoiding sabre-tooth tigers in the last Ice Age, but not so much when booking a year-long luxury trip around the world.

Knowing this gives you the power to move towards your desires, even if you feel fearful. Don't deny your feelings, but use them as a powerful stepping stone to move forward instead.

When I work with my clients one-to-one, I have the powerful ability to help them shift through these perceived limitations. Through a powerful mix of mindset, energy work, structures and support, I help them to shift out of their overworking pattern to a new way of living - "work 2.0", as I like to call it. In work 2.0, ease, rest, fun, flow and fulfilment are some of the most important elements when creating a successful life.

During my coaching sessions, I let your body's natural intuition direct us where to go. As we are looking into your current stumbling block, we use a technique I like to describe as "let your body tell the story". Things like back pain, tightness in the chest and a blockage in the throat area are some of the most common sensations that I work with. Let me give you an example to help explain what I mean.

My client Jane was struggling with overwhelm during the events of 2020. As she was stripped of all her freedoms and was bound to her home, she was starting to get extremely anxious. Out of fear of losing all her clients and not being able to pay the bills, she accepted a lot of PITA (Pain In The Ass) clients. These clients drained her even further, resulting in Jane's health taking a real hit. This downward spiral prompted her to reach out to me, and together we created a plan to get her back on track with her amazing business.

During our sessions, it became clear that Jane was struggling for the common reasons that I explained in the previous chapter. Her body was showing signs of tiredness, overwhelm, confusion, heaviness, PMS problems, etc. As we started diving into the beliefs to clear these heavy sensations from her body, it became clear that a lot of her experiences were tied to childhood memories and generational patterns.

Getting to the core of each belief allowed us to shift her current struggles quickly, and replace her unhelpful (generational) beliefs with 21st century beliefs that served her and her business better. I am happy to report that she is doing a lot better now, and is learning to set better boundaries and leave the PITA clients in the past.

Now, if you are new to the self-help thing, you may be thinking: Susanne, what the hell is a belief? A belief is nothing more than a thought you keep repeating to yourself. It may be something you keep actively saying, or something you accept as the truth inside of your body, and don't even notice that you have accepted it as the truth within.

To give you a few examples of beliefs:

- Life is meant to be hard
- I need to work hard to receive
- I need to be busy to feel good enough
- Unless I do x, y and z my parents/partner/children won't love me

These I would class as personal beliefs. Things you believe, for you, as a person to be true. We also experience something called cultural beliefs on a daily basis. A cultural belief is something that depends on the culture or area you grew up in. For example in Japan black cats are considered lucky, while in the USA black cats are considered to bring bad luck.

Cultural beliefs also tie in with what I like to call generational beliefs. These beliefs are passed down through your family or the culture you grew up in and this again shapes who you are as a person. When working with clients who struggle with overworking, they are often operating on generational beliefs that hard work pays off. To give you an example, your (great) grandfather worked hard to rebuild the country after the Second World

War. It is possible he believed that working hard is necessary to be successful.

Such information gets stored in our bodies and passed down through the generations. It is referred to as epigenetics. The environment can cause changes in your behaviour and affect the way your genes work. These are not permanent changes and it won't alter your DNA sequence. But they can change how your body reads a DNA sequence. See these experiences as a light switch. Through the year some light switches are turned on, some are turned off, but the good news is, you get to decide what stays on and off. In order words, these changes can be reversed. This is exactly what I help my clients with.

All of these beliefs come together within your body as you get to decide which ones apply to your life. So in the example given, do you believe black cats bring you good or bad luck? Our body stores thousands upon thousands of beliefs that together make the mixture of you. That's why if you find yourself stuck it might not even be something you believe in, but it may be the result of a belief that is passed down through your body instead. Mind-blowing right?

When you know what you are looking for it is quite easy to make these changes within our beliefs. If you want my help making these changes, feel free to have a look at the resources page of the book.

Understanding how your body is designed to work helps you move out of Struggle Town for good. To shift into the new exciting reality where the struggle is a thing of the past and you align yourself with ease, fun and flow, we need to do some digging on limiting beliefs. You don't need to drag up the traumatic past and relive all kinds of bad memories - you just need to understand what you believe to be true about success.

Again, this is not meant to make you miserable for days; it is just to create awareness around where you are, so you know in what direction you are going. View this exercise as an objective experience, where you are just taking stock of old experiences, beliefs and situations.

I like to imagine myself travelling through time, visiting my younger self as it allows me to stay objective, and give her a loving hand just in case she needs me.

It's time to journal on the following questions:

- When I think about success, what comes to mind?

- When I think about these memories, what do I feel in my body?

- Why do I believe I can't have what I want?

- What makes me think I am not good enough / not worthy of having the success I desire?

This could look something like this:

When I think about success it reminds me of the time when I won an award for the best drawing in kindergarten. My sister got really upset with me for getting the attention she wanted, and broke my trophy. The story I told myself is that I was better off not doing anything I love, otherwise the people I love will get upset with me.

Thinking back about this, this memory makes my stomach twist. I want to create a life full of success and things I enjoy, but I also don't want to upset my family, and feel like I did when I was six years old.

Keep going until you've gone through all the questions. This may take a few pages, so you may want to take a few days to write this out. Just keep writing until you feel you are getting close to the core of your beliefs. No need to edit, just free write that shit, no one is watching!

As you are writing you probably are starting to see certain patterns and beliefs you adopted when you were growing up.

Things like "if I succeed, people will be jealous", or "if I get what I want, there isn't enough for other people". Remember it is important to acknowledge where you are at, and honour what it is you are feeling - but you don't need to go digging into it and fixing stuff. You've got places to be and shit to get done.

You will also notice that your head might start reasoning with you: *"but when X happened, of course I felt like that. Anyone would feel that way."* This is completely normal; just acknowledge it, allow yourself to feel what you feel, and write it down. Remember you are in a safe space and there is no need to hide who you are when you are hanging out in my universe.

Now let's journal on the next questions:

- When I was taught that success only meant money/fame/followers on social media/relationships, how did that make me feel?

- When I think about these memories, what conclusions did I draw about what success means to me or should mean to me?

- Is it really true that this belief/these beliefs about success are my only option, or could something else be true? Hint: there are always other options!

Keep going until you feel you reach the core of your success story. It shouldn't take more than a few hours, so if you tend to overdo these things, just set your alarm on your phone and be done when it buzzes.

If you are like me, or any other human being on this planet, you might start telling yourself that you are stuck or don't know how to do this as part of your limiting beliefs around success. The thing is, if you knew how to get to the success you desire and deserve in life, you would've done it by now. It is why you picked up this book in the first place. So if you don't know how to do this yet, you are in the right place.

We don't get taught how to listen to our bodies when growing up. Instead, we get told to listen to others and authority figures like parents, teachers and doctors. As I am now officially a grown-up (although I can't say I feel like one every day of the week), it is safe to say that many of us have no clue what we are doing, and all we can do sometimes is wing it and hope for the best. If you've given your power away to the adults in your life, and maybe still assume they know better, it is time to claim back that part of yourself and *trust* that you can figure this out.

If you find it difficult to think of all of the answers to these questions, I need you to take a couple of deep breaths and shift your focus from your head to your heart (literally just feel your heart area). This allows you to go from thinking about these questions to feeling about these questions. And as you allow yourself to feel into this, you will get the answers you need, I promise you. If you need a bit of extra support, listen to the meditation from the resources first before starting journaling, or sign up for my free *Lifestyle Design Masterclass* in the resources.

Remember that with any new skill, it takes practice. So if you are new to journaling, or tuning in to your body and emotions, give yourself a break and just do the best you can. You didn't learn how to walk in one go, how to talk in a day, or how to read all of these words in just a few tries either.

Now are you ready to get to all the yummy goodness life has to offer?

It's time to journal on a few more:

- Think about the life you want and answer the following question: what would I like to achieve?

  Break it down into three steps: (1) short-term (next few weeks); (2) mid-term (next few months); and (3) long-term (stuff I really want, but it's fine if it happens in the next year or so). Then say why you want it, and most of all why you *deserve* it. If you don't know why, remember that you *are*, so therefore you are worthy.

Be as creative as you like, and embrace this process. Prefer visuals? Use journals that are available to purchase from the website. You can also make your own dream board or start pinning stuff on Pinterest. Do whatever you need to do to make you feel good about your goals. If it doesn't make you feel good, pick something else. Your feelings are the indicator that you are on the right track.

If you want some more feel-good music to help you get in the mood and shake your booty all day long, remember to get the book resources at http://dropthestruggle.co.uk/ as I've created a fun YouTube playlist for you. It has all my favourite tracks - I add more regularly - and you also have access to meditation to help you focus on your future reality and connect with the feel-good zone.

Now you know where you are and where you want to go, it's time to learn to apply your personalised success strategy. I'm so excited! Are you? I'll see you in the next chapter...

Your Success Strategy

"There is a powerful driving force inside every human being that, once unleashed, can make any vision, dream, or desire a reality."

Anthony Robbins

The way you define success is unique to your upbringing and your experience, as we've discovered in the previous chapters. This definition can make or break your success in life, and is very important to your current success strategy. Do you think success comes easy? Or do you have to work hard? Does success show itself in all areas of your life? Or can you only have it in one or two areas, whilst the rest stays behind?

Through the years, I've noticed distinct differences between my clients. However, they all seem to fit into four different categories, or archetypes, as I like to call them. To help you get clear on your success strategy, I would like to use this opportunity to help you unravel yours.

If you don't know your success strategy yet, please visit my website and take my free and fun 60-second quiz to help you get started. You can find the quiz at <u>grantmethod.com/quiz</u>.

Knowing your success strategy allows you to easily start breaking these patterns that are keeping you stuck, in a way that is aligned with who you really are.

The Nurturer

The first type I call the nurturer. If you are a nurturer, you are a very caring person, who supports, protects and cares for others. You want to grow your business and have more success. However, you are still in the early stages or struggling to take your business to the next level. But you are committed to making this work. You just don't know how.

You are an amazing person who likes to make a difference in people's lives. So big kudos to you for trying to make a change. However, on the flip side, you can find yourself overwhelmed at times. Too many ideas, too much to do, too much responsibility, and too little time to make it all happen. And that can make you feel incredibly frustrated.

You can feel that the people you care about are standing in the way of your success. This can lead to you feeling resentful and irritated because no one seems to notice or give a damn about the sacrifices you make.

My client Jane is a nurturer. She came to me a few months ago completely burned out. As a single mum of a child with special needs, she knew she was spreading herself way too thin. Jane had a coaching business that was doing well, but with all the clients, admin, appointments for her daughter, she was at her wit's end.

During our first strategy session, it became clear that Jane did not have a clear system to manage all her daily tasks. And she just kind of winged it, hoping for the best each day. Taking a step back from the business allowed her to streamline the onboarding process for clients, set up a booking system, and outsource simple repetitive tasks to her VA. This resulted in her reducing her working hours by ten hours a week, which allowed her to get enough sleep again, and get herself organised each week. She happily shared with me the other day how great it is to be able to spend the time with her daughter, as well as enjoy the freedom her business now gives her.

The Explorer

If you are an explorer, you are a powerful and driven person with a great vision. You have a lot of ideas and you are often very creative, sometimes through art but especially through the way you express yourself in your business. You are a creative powerhouse that likes to make a change in this world with the amazing work you do.

However, you can find yourself overwhelmed at times, just like the nurturer. Because you don't have a clear strategy yet, you are looking around and searching for an answer, in a place outside of yourself. If you are in business, you are experiencing some level of success, but something is missing, but you just don't know what exactly. This can bring up some frustration, combined with feelings of tiredness and overwhelm.

My client Claire is a typical explorer. She loved her work as a designer, but because her creativity drives her and her business, she is always ready to explore more. Claire kept buying more online courses, especially during lockdown. But because she was too busy, those were still sitting unused on her digital bookshelf.

Claire reached out to me after hearing me speak about mental health and alignment on a podcast. On this podcast, I explained why having a clear strategy to grow your business is a better strategy than the "work hard and hustle" culture that is widely promoted. Growing her creative business always came through hard work, so she was intrigued to find out more. In her breakthrough session, we discovered a deep childhood belief of never being good enough and having to constantly prove herself. This belief was now her internal motivator to show the world what she was made of. Hence her overworking pattern.

During our coaching sessions, we tweaked this belief so it would include rest and self-care as part of her long-term success strategy. When I told her I was writing this book, she told me to share that her business has grown by twenty percent, and she is feeling great on top of that. She recently started dating an amazing guy, something she previously didn't believe she had time for.

The Hero

Type number three I call the hero. You are a superhero, a warrior and you know how to get things done. This means you have great success with your business and you find that you hit your targets pretty easily. But you want more. More reach, more impact, more success - and you are ready to go after it.

But you keep being too busy for this, because you are constantly trying to prove your worth. And let's be honest here, no matter how hard you try, or how much you do, there is always that feeling that there is never enough time to do everything you want to do, isn't there?

My client Jack and his wife Amber worked with me together to better navigate their extremely busy lives. Both Jack and Amber were CEOs and felt they were in high demand, having to be available for the business 24/7. As we started working together it became clear that both of them were operating on belief systems that were passed down through their family lines. The belief "work hard and you will be successful" is very common, but it was driving a wedge between them, and their marriage was starting to break down because of it.

Due to their busy schedules, they rarely spent quality time together. While working together, we managed to re-organise these schedules so there was plenty of time for each other. They started going for daily walks together in the mornings, instead of exercising separately. Once a week they had an evening together and once a month they would travel to the countryside. For this high-achieving couple their lifestyle is still very busy, but their relationship is no longer suffering now they've found a way that works for them.

The Rebel

If your results from the quiz say that you are a rebel, it means you are very successful by society's norms. You have worked yourself to the top and you are a valuable player in your field of expertise. You are not scared of working hard and long hours. You are very proud of how far you've come and how much you've accomplished. This means you live a full-on life and you go all in and that you experience great (financial) success and you experience what society calls "having it all".

However, there are days you struggle with your emotions and your physical health (things like PMS, back pains and/or sleepless nights). You feel guilty at times for "having it all" but it is still not good enough. And no matter how hard you work, or how much you do, you are not able to shake that "it's not good enough" feeling. This leads to you doing more as you hate feeling powerless.

This never-ending circle is a guaranteed way to epically screw over yourself, your relationships, your health and your business. You know you cannot continue living the way you did before, because you can feel that your body is about to throw in the towel.

My client Lorraine came to me after a massive health scare. She was recently hospitalised after she collapsed during a board meeting and was diagnosed with an uncomplicated heart attack. This was her sign from the universe it was time for a change ASAP.

It became clear that Lorraine was pushing herself way too hard. When we did our first strategy session and calculated how much time all her to-dos took each week, we discovered she was almost 50 hours too short. Of course, because she had much more to do than the hours in the day allowed her, she was trying to push herself very hard. But it was simply impossible for any human being to achieve such an enormous task. This was an eye-opening epiphany moment for her. Because she was still on sick leave as the board insisted on her fully recovering before returning back to work, we managed to completely redesign her life in the meantime.

We worked closely together for a year, to avoid her filling up her schedule when she was back at work. Lorraine had to learn how to stop micromanaging in every area of her life and allow her team to support her. By doing so, she took the pressure off herself, and both her doctor and Lorraine herself are happy to report that she is doing great.

Being successful or having the impact you desire, doesn't mean working more hours or running yourself into the ground. It's about implementing a strategy that allows you to take your business from successful to phenomenal.

So based on your results from the quiz that you can find at grantmethod.com/quiz, what type are you? Does the description resonate with you? What do you believe to be true about success? Can you have it all? Or does it come through hard work only? Does it feel limited and restricted? Or do you feel successful most - if not all - of the time?

We are told so many myths and lies about success. For you to create that outrageously amazing life you want - and deserve - we need to tackle the common untruths about success that we are supposed to believe. We will do this in the next chapter, so you can start living your outrageously successful life now!

Myths About Success

"Feel the fear. Have the doubts. Go for It anyway."

Barbara Stanny

When I started my coaching business in 2015, I was a 29-year old mum to a one-year-old baby trying to create my dream life through my business. Until then, I dreamed of becoming financially independent and having the freedom to spend my time any way I desired.

Now, six years later, at the time of writing this, I'm reaping the benefits of the seeds I sowed all those years ago. Today I have an award-winning coaching business, host sold-out masterminds, and events, and my work has often been featured in the media. But this success didn't come overnight: first I had to get rid of a lot of limiting beliefs that no longer served me and my goals.

I've made many mistakes along the way. For example, not managing to have the success I desired in the early years, and spending so many hours wondering what to do to make my business a success (and what I was doing wrong). Or worse, what was wrong with *me*.

To allow yourself to kick your unsuccessful habits to the curb once and for all, it is important to discuss the biggest myths about success. Why? Because once you have the awareness about the limiting stories you tell yourself, you can decide to write a different ending.

So let's dive into the biggest myths we have been told about having the success you desire and deserve.

Myth 1 - Success require sacrifice

Even though it's promoted as the thing to do, to work hard, hustle, work until you drop, sacrifice everything you have and keep going until you make it to the top, it is not a great long-term and sustainable strategy for you or your business. It is also not a requirement to succeed. If you plan to be in business for a long time, draining yourself energetically, spiritually, emotionally and mentally is not a solid, long-term success strategy.

For you to become the best you can be, you need to apply a strategy that is in alignment with who you are (as discussed in the previous chapter), what you desire, and what kind of impact you want to have. You don't have to work yourself to a breakdown to prove you are worthy and dedicated. You are most effective when your cup is full and overflowing. Create a business and life that supports that vision. You matter!

Myth 2 - Success is linear

Any business owner or CEO knows success isn't linear. It goes up and down, and yet it's not something we openly talk about. We talk about the successes, talk about the quest, talk about the exciting journey suggesting success is linear, but it comes with lows and highs.

If you are experiencing setbacks in your business, it's not because there's something wrong with you. It is just a normal part of what it means to run your own business. Not everyone will understand this, especially if they don't have their own business themselves. If you are struggling to navigate this, make sure to use the resources in this book to support you through this.

Myth 3 - Failure should be taken personally

When things come crashing down, it can feel very overwhelming. However, failure is feedback, not a death sentence or a self-worth assessment. If you are in business as a solopreneur or business owner, or if you run a big company as the CEO, it is hard not to take things personally when things don't go as planned. Of course, you feel responsible for the choices you made and the staff you employ.

You are responsible for the choices made, but you should not internalise your mistakes. More often than not, it's not the end of the world when things go differently than expected. In most cases, it's a redirect to something better. Try to separate the two.

I know this one is tricky as we are taught to take responsibility for our actions. But if stuff does come crashing down, it is sometimes better to just let the pieces fall and minimise the damage, rather than trying to fight the process. And to be honest, the periods in my life where I felt things were falling apart, they were falling together (and by the way, this tied in with my personal belief that things had to be hard for me to receive anything).

Myth 4 - Being busy equals being productive

As a coach myself working with busy people, I see this happen all the time. We put endless things on our to-do list. We "should" be doing all these things because that is what is expected of us. Or so we think. We wear so many hats, from running your business and being a partner, parent, friend - you name it.

Yet being productive is something completely different to being busy. So if you're talking about success, are the things you're working on actually part of your long-term strategy to create those dreams and hit those targets? Or are you just keeping yourself busy for the sake of being busy because it makes you feel important?

Next time you plan activities, make your to-do lists and fill up your calendar, think about the following questions. Do these things contribute to my vision for myself, my family, and my business? Am I productive, or am I just keeping myself busy with things I should be doing?

If you often find yourself on the hamster wheel of endless to-do's, keep reading. In the final chapters I will give you some great tips to navigate this much more effectively.

Myth 5 - Rest is overrated

We live in a society that values doing over being. We are taught to just go, go, go and get things done. Hit those targets and get towards those goals with as much speed and force as we can.

Looking after yourself is equally, if not more, important to achieving your goals, and is a vital part of becoming the most successful version of yourself that you can possibly be. There is no point trying to build your business at the expense of your marriage or working yourself into burnout, as you wouldn't even get to enjoy what you've created.

Therefore, rest is a productivity activity, because you know that you can get much more done - and do it better - after a good night's sleep than if you haven't slept for a night or two or three. Well-being matters for you, and the people you work with, and once you start prioritising how you feel, you will notice a drastic improvement in all areas of your life and business. So success comes with plenty of time to rest, recharge and realign for the best - and easiest - results.

There is nothing wrong with doing what you love and bringing your vision to life. But real success isn't just a number in your bank account. It's how you feel inside when you look at yourself in the mirror, or the things you tell yourself late at night. Success can come without sacrifice if you are willing to change how you spend your time, and rewrite what you were made to believe growing up.

These core elements show that real, sustainable long-term success, wellbeing, health and wealth start by adopting an all-inclusive work-life balance vision that serves you, your family, and your business.

Myth 6 - Time equals money

When this is one of the beliefs that is running the show, you will struggle with scaling your business past a certain point. Do you keep hitting the same income goals? Or the same number of clients? The chances are that you believe time equals money.

We live in an era where we can create money on autopilot with the right marketing strategy, and generate what is called *passive income* - so if you are ready to expand your business but are not managing, look into this belief first. Time doesn't have to equal money.

Myth 7 - Multitasking improves productivity

Busted! This myth is one of the biggest lies many of us have to cope with. Multitasking does not improve your productivity. Research shows the opposite. If you stop multitasking, you will increase your productivity by 40 percent.

Learn to focus your time singularly. Focus on one thing at a time and get it done. Always start with the task that will create the biggest momentum for your business. Ask yourself this question each morning: what is the number #1 thing I can do today that has the biggest ROI? Break it down, plan it, and take action.

Myth 8 - Planning is pointless

Proper preparation is a real time saver. When you find yourself overwhelmed with all the to-do's, planning and preparing can feel like a waste of time. However, if you take a step back, take a bird's eye view and observe how to move forward, you will gain the upper hand. Make time each month, each week and each day to make a plan - going from general goals to specifics - and slay those goals with ease as you have clarity once again!

Myth 9 - Time is linear

Have you ever noticed that the way you feel about time differs depending on the situation? Some days time feels like it flies by, and other days it feels like it's going so incredibly slowly. Did you ever wonder what makes time slow down for you? Start noticing your patterns. Why? Your perception of time can be changed. When you know what makes time slow down for you, you can start applying it when you need it the most.

All of these myths can influence you to some degree, and make it difficult to break free and move forward towards your dreams. So now we have busted all these myths, let's uncover the biggest success killers.

Success Killers

"Whether you come from a council estate or a country estate, your success will be determined by your own confidence and fortitude."

Michelle Obama

When it comes to creating the success you desire many blocks can show themselves. If you go back to your journal and read through your answers, you will see a clear pattern occurring. What is your go-to response which keeps telling you you can't have the success you desire? Have a look now before we continue, as it will help you let go of this belief right now.

Working with my clients from all over the world and from all different backgrounds, many blocks seem to transcend cultural differences. Again, creating awareness around why you are keeping yourself stuck will help you move forward towards creating a new life that is filled with everything your heart desires.

These are the most common blocks I've uncovered for myself and my clients.

I don't have the time

Oh, if I got a nickel for every time I'd heard this phrase! The truth is "I don't have the time" can mean a lot of different things. On top of that, it is a socially acceptable excuse to not participate in something.

But it is not about having the time; it is about creating the time for things that matter to you. If you really want to move towards this, you will find a way. If not you will find an excuse.

Especially as women, we are conditioned to be people-pleasers. We are supposed to say "yes" even if we don't want to, or if it doesn't serve us. Otherwise we're a bitch, right?

The thing is, if you really want to start creating a life that lights your soul and puts that fire in your belly, you have to start treating the time you've got differently.

We all have the same amount of hours each week. Yet some of us seem to be able to move mountains, and others struggle their way through it. If you are serious about changing this, I need you to decide, right here, right now, that this is what you want.

How does that feel to you, knowing from now on you will make the time for that thing you desire? Does it feel overwhelming? Impossibile? Sit with this feeling for a bit and journal on it if you feel that would help.

Once you've decided you want to start moving towards your new successes, you don't have to see it as "I have to move this mountain" and work hard.

I am sure you can find five minutes this week to move towards what you desire. Do you spend a lot of time watching TV or Netflix? Before you turn that on today, put your energy towards that dream of yours. Just dream about it for a few minutes! Have a google to see if you can find more information.

Maybe tell a supportive friend that you want to get a degree, take a course, or write a book. You can make time here and there to help your desires come true.

If you can find five minutes, how about an hour? Can you plan for an hour this week to dive in deeper? How about an hour each day?

Whatever works well for you, make the time for it. Plan it into your calendar, use your phone, set reminders and break that pattern and your excuses of not having the time. You can have the success you want. You decide.

I don't know how or I don't know where to start

Newsflash, no one does. But I promise you, everything is figureoutable. Everything you see around you, from the TV you watch to the phone you hold and the book you are reading right now, everything was once a thought, a dream, an insight from someone (or a lot of people together). These words that I am writing, the book, kindle or phone you are reading these words on, even the words I am using, were all once made up by someone and brought into this reality.

Using the "I don't know how" excuse can keep you stuck for a long time, because you will not find the answer you are looking for on the same frequency as the question.

Imagine your desire is a radio, with the tuner set on 96 FM but you want to reach 101.2 FM because that's where the solution, the goal is. If you keep focusing on 96 FM, you will never hear what is on the other channel.

You don't need to know how or where to start. That is what the universe is for, as explained in chapter 3 (more on that later).

But remember, for every problem, there is a solution. It is up to you to decide where you want to focus your energy.

Fear of [insert your favourite excuse]

Fear is a tricky motherfucker. It is helpful in some situations to keep you safe, but most of the time this is what keeps you stuck.

Whether it is fear of success, fear of missing out, fear of failure, fear of not being good enough, it all comes down to you not fully trusting yourself yet, and knowing you have the power to create the life and success you desire.

Remember, I am not asking you to climb a mountain. I am asking you to take the next step. Do you think you can put one foot in front of the other and figure it out as you go?

The other day I was in the park with my seven-year-old daughter. She kept insisting on climbing up one of the most impractical and highest slides, even though it scares the bejeebers out of her.

As she climbed up once more she started to panic, putting her feet in the wrong places, holding her breath and pushing herself up at the wrong times.

In her panicky voice she shouted at me: "Mama, I'm scared"! I heard myself reply to her: "I know you are, but that doesn't mean you can't do it. Deep breaths, refocus and you've got this!"

She pulled herself together and pushed herself up, only seconds after me telling her she can be scared and still succeed. Afterwards, she came to me and said: "Mama, I found it really scary but I think I did a fantastic job, and really enjoyed it once I got the hang of it." Lesson: you can be scared and still do a great job.

I don't believe I am good enough or worthy

I've struggled with not feeling worthy for a long time. Every now and then it still peeps up to tell me all kinds of shit that isn't true. Want to know the real truth? You are worthy because you are.

It is that simple. You are worthy because you are alive, here on this planet, living and breathing. You don't need to do anything, you don't need to be anything, you don't need to have a certain number in your bank account. When all of that gets stripped away and you are left with absolutely nothing, it still applies. You are worthy. Period.

Any other thought or feeling you tell yourself that is the opposite of this is simply not true. It may be something someone told you in the past, or a frequency you tapped into by accident. Call yourself out on the bullshit stories you tell yourself because nothing couldn't be further from the truth. You are an amazing, beautiful person, and you are worthy beyond measure. And that's all you need to know.

Not believing you can have it

For centuries women have been told that we should know our place, stay in our lane. Don't speak up, keep yourself small, no one wants your opinion. Equal rights, the right to vote? Don't be crazy. And yet, all of these dreams of the women before us are now the reality.

There is still plenty that needs to be done, but that being said, you have the power to make that change. You are powerful and you can take back the power that you were convinced to give away. The power to create life is your birthright, and no one can take that power away from you unless you give it away.

Journaling questions:

As we are getting closer to the end of this book, it is important to start shifting from your past beliefs to your current and future reality. Now we've busted all the myths and limitations, it is time to start applying this information to your specific situation. Please journal on the following questions in preparation for the final chapters.

- Looking back at my journaling answers from previous chapters, I am now realising: *(journal on any ahas and insights you've received)*

- Knowing that I can decide any time to make a change to my current situation, what feelings/fears/worries come to mind?

- As I get to decide what I believe to be true, what beliefs would feel better to start repeating from now on? For example:
    - *I don't need to do everything by myself*
    - *I don't need to know how to change this (the universe takes care of that for me); I just need to focus on what I do want, instead of what I don't want,*
    - *I am good enough*
    - *I didn't know how to be more successful, but as I am reading this book I am starting to figure it out, now that I am changing my beliefs. There comes a point where I will completely understand this new concept. It's just like a muscle: I am practising it to get stronger and stronger.*

- My current reality is a reflection of what I (used to) believe. I wonder how great my life will be. I am thinking I can change:..... (*fill in the blank - just keep writing for a few minutes and let things flow*)

As we are now moving away from the struggle part of your life, I recommend you start listening to the guided meditation daily. If you haven't done so yet, you can access your free resources at http://dropthestruggle.co.uk/.

Being Comfortable With Success

"The secret, Alice, is to surround yourself with people who make your heart smile. It's then, only then, that you'll find Wonderland."

Lewis Carroll, Alice In Wonderland

Celebrating your success publicly can be one of the most terrifying things you will ever do (I know, I know, what an opening!). But if we don't address the elephant in the room there is no point in me writing this book and sharing my best secrets with you. So why are we, as a society, uncomfortable with success?

It is a tricky question that will require us to go deeper into the conditioning each of us has experienced growing up. For example, I was born and bred in The Netherlands, and in the Dutch language, there are many different sayings that suggest that standing out, raising your head above everyone else was something you shouldn't do, as it could cost you your head.

In high school I was named one of the honour students, because of the work I'd done for the other students throughout the years, and making the school a more pleasant environment for all of us. One of the previous winners was upset with receiving this honour, saying that "by singling out one of us you take away from the others". Her strong response to something that was such an honour for me, made me wonder about how we each see success in different ways.

For me, sharing my success, especially on dark days, is like letting in a glorious ray of sunshine. I am standing there, tall and proud, shining my light into this world and by doing so, I am allowing others to do the same. I am not taking away anything from you. I am the light. I am showing you my success and my failures, so you realise that what I've got, you can have too.

However, this previous winner didn't believe that there was an unlimited light to be shared, and putting her in the spotlight meant everyone else had to sit in the dark. But that is not how light works.

Even if we can't physically see the light shine, it resonates all around us. From a quantum physics perspective (as explained in the third chapter) this light - your light - will always shine and reach even the furthest corners of the universe. Now, isn't that good to know.

Another example. After I finished my bachelor's degree I joined the master's programme *Holocaust and Genocide* to write a thesis on the family of my best friend. Something I've dreamed of doing ever since he and I met many years before. This master's allowed me to dive deep into the history of some of the biggest genocides (like the witch trials) and uncover why we behave in a certain way under pressure. This turned out to be extremely beneficial, as I am now working with clients on deep generational trauma and limiting beliefs around success. This is often rooted in these life-changing events our families endured.

In 2011 I finished writing a beautiful thesis about the Dutch resistance, this specific family and the sacrifices they made. Because I've written a few articles about it which are available online (including footnotes and references) to this day, it is still getting the attention from current students and researchers. And there isn't a year that goes by without me receiving another request from someone asking if they can get a copy of my thesis. As a matter of fact, I received another request from France as I was writing this book. Isn't that a coincidence? The point being, don't underestimate how big of an impact your contribution means to the bigger picture.

Your work, your life, you, everything about you. It all matters. And the impact you are having, have had and can have is beyond anything you can imagine. Knowing that you are fully loved and supported by the universe / divine / god / higher self / angels / however you call it is such an amazing feeling. And with that knowledge, you can now take a deep breath, relax those shoulders and know you've got this.

As I've explained before, everything is made of energy and every thought is too. Every thought ever thought still exists to this day on a vibrational level in this ever expanding universe. That's why you may resonate with more negative beliefs (including those from others) than you realise. From things we go through growing up to the messages we receive from the media or through our upbringing, there are all kinds of energetics involved when you are trying to buy a one-way ticket out of Struggle Town.

Now, we could go digging for days, months or even years and spend tons of time, money and energy on making sense of all these experiences. Of course, it is helpful for you to understand and have the awareness of where you are at (hence me writing about this in the previous chapters), but you don't need to spend years on figuring out all of these patterns, beliefs and triggers of dead ancestors. I see this a lot in the entrepreneurial space, especially when working in the mindset and spiritual healing space as we are doing here together. Trust me, if you want to move forward it is not necessary to keep digging into your past and everything you did "wrong".

In a world where everything is energy and every thought still exists, it is up to us what we align ourselves with. Because we are made of energy and are conscious beings, we can create by focusing our energy anywhere we want it to be. That's why the law of attraction is such an amazing - and sometimes a very annoying - supporter, because it will always bring you more of what you are sending out into the universe. But if you want the success you are after, you have to place your alignment before action *every time* so you can bring your future reality to the now.

Creating the success you desire starts by realising that you are worthy of anything you desire in life. You are worthy of your success because you are part of this ever-expanding universe. You don't need to prove anything, you don't need to do anything, you don't need to act a certain way or be a certain way. You are allowed to receive anything you want because you exist. Or simply put, you are always supported, no matter what.

When realising we have the power to create what we want, I often get the question: what about all the bad things that have happened to me or other people? Unfortunately, I don't know how to answer this question for you, because I've gone through my fair share of shit in life and no matter how hard you try you cannot make sense of non-sense. I don't know why my mother groped me, why my ex-boyfriend cheated or why that guy choked me. I can think about it until the cows come home but what happened will never be okay.

If shit like that happens, what can you do? You can decide something will destroy you (been there for sure) or it can be the stepping stone for something better. For example, going through these ordeals made me passionate about equal rights, mental health and creating real health and wealth for others. Those desires were born out of these "bad experiences". You get to decide where you keep giving the power to what happened to you in the past or if you are using it as fuel to create something new or better. And if you are not managing to find closure on something that happened to you, just get the support you deserve to make this easier on you. You are worth it. Give yourself permission to take the road of least resistance.

So how do you start being comfortable with success when things haven't been flowing the way you desire for years, if not decades? Or a better question is: how do you start having more success much easier?

When you start embodying that new feeling of success, you must start practising this daily. As I explained before, we've experienced generations of "stay small", "be invisible" or "don't brag" conditioning to deal with before celebrating your awesomeness will be the new norm. Which can make you feel uncomfortable, to begin with. Just stick with it, it will get easier the more you do it.

I recommend you use the *Drop The Motherfucking Struggle Journals* to help you start celebrating with yourself. As you get more comfortable sharing your successes with yourself (and tooting your own horn and blowing your own trumpet) you can start sharing it with other people. Tell them about this book and your exciting new ideas.

You can also share your successes with me on social media by tagging me in your posts (links are in the resources section) and adding the hashtags #dtmfs or #dropthestruggle. If you are not ready to share it publicly yet, you can also email me and my team at love@reachsusanne.com. We would love to hear from you.

The more and more you practice, the easier it will become. You feel more at ease with the success within as you recognise your awesomeness and brilliance, you will start seeing more and more of that reflected in your outside world too. Remember, it's just like a muscle. Keep practising!

But how does success feel, and how do you fully embody everything your heart desires? Let me take you through my five-step success formula in the next chapter to help you make your wildest dreams come true.

But first, let's journal on the following questions, so you know what you want to create moving forward.

Journaling Questions:

- What is good in my life?

  Things like: I love the comfy bed, fresh air, my partner, my body, my phone, this beautiful notebook. Anything you can feel, see or touch around you that feels good.

- What am I proud of today?

  Did you do anything that makes you feel proud? Did your feet take you where you wanted to go or did they wander off without you? Did you have food to eat? Fresh water to drink? Daylight to enjoy? And in particular, find something that you can positively say about yourself. For example, I tried my best today, and I know I will try again tomorrow. I love how inventive I am and I know I can figure it out.

- Knowing I am fully supported by my soul, spirit and the universe, what else I am grateful for, knowing it is all coming my way?

Write about future experiences feeling as if they already happened. I am so grateful for releasing my blocks and shifting into a life that is much more fun and flowy. I so appreciate knowing I am supported, and I can feel it most of the time. If I forget there is always something or someone who pops up and reminds me. I keep seeing all these number sequences like 11.11 and 12.34, which are the angels letting me know they are here and they too are supporting and guiding me. I know I can have anything I want, and I choose to create what I truly want. And if something does come up that I don't like, I know that it is just for me to appreciate the contrast and remind myself what I do want, because I get to decide what I focus on. I am so so grateful for myself, my body and the universe allowing me to bring my wildest dreams to life.

Remember to listen to the guided meditation daily as this allows you to make this process as easy as possible.

Embodying Your Success

"Opportunities don't happen. You create them."

Chris Grosser

As we discovered in the previous chapter, the definition of success differs depending on how you were raised, and what things you were exposed to growing up. Redefining what success means to you is the missing key to creating an outrageously successful life and business. But how does success feel to you? What does it mean to you to be successful? What does it mean to you to know you can achieve anything your heart desires?

Success to me means knowing I am fully supported, trusting myself and the universe to co-create this together, and knowing at the same time there will always be more I want to do, be or have. This perfect state, this balance where I am grateful for what I have and have created, knowing that I am on my way to more, is what makes me feel like I am right where I am meant to be.

Knowing I cannot fail as I am deeply guided by my higher self, God, the universe or divine (whatever word resonates best with you) and that any setback is just a plot twist that will bring me even more of the things I desire (but didn't know I wanted).

My client Sarah experienced this shift first hand and is the perfect example. Sarah, just like my other clients, was used to working hard, putting in long hours and making stuff happen. Now she is a mother, she started to see these overworking patterns back with her young children.

Self-care was pretty much non-existent and her health was starting to decline as she was suffering from sleepless nights, anxiety and recently also panic attacks. I helped Sarah to shift her beliefs around the *perception of time* and *sacrifice to receive*, implementing new structures and systems in her business that supported her goals, as well as working on the alignment piece before taking further action.

Not long after she and I started working together, she landed three extra clients. She didn't have to hustle or chase them down, they just reached out to her.

That's why it is so important to work on the frequency you send out to the universe. You cannot receive things easily if you believe it has to be hard. But as she and I shifted these patterns through the transformational coaching sessions, different situations started to show up, proving to her that it was indeed possible to have an easier life. And if she and I can do it, you can do so too.

There are three important steps we need to help you figure out, to help you create the life you desire:

- Create awareness of where your current limits are. Uncover your current set point or conditioning so you know where you are (thanks to the previous journal exercises).

- Peel away the layers of all your perceived limitations to get to the real you underneath. You are worthy beyond measure. You are deeply loved and supported. From there, you can start thinking and visualising what it is you want to create.

- Decide. Make the decision, take a stand and claim what it is you want to create. You have free will in this universe and if you want things to be easier from now on, you can decide this right here and now. Know that you are 100 percent supported, and no idea is too much or too "out there". So what do you want to do with your life moving forward? Be as crazy as you want to be. You cannot fail. Be brave, state what you want. Say it loud and proud. You get to decide. So decide now and let's do this!

Creating a business and the success that comes along with it can be one of the most exhilarating feelings in the world. Besides the obvious side effects of having a successful business, such as revenue and the number of people helped, there are other benefits such as promotions, awards, or ways to grow and stretch ourselves personally in more ways than you can imagine.

When getting to the next level of success in your business, it is important to ask yourself what this success entails. Questions like "what does success look like to me" or "what goals do I want to achieve" need to be clear in your mind. But, you have already decided on these new goals you want to achieve next. How do you create these new *experiences*?

I've seen my clients successfully hit their goals easily by implementing my five-step process after being stuck on the same level for a long time. It is such an amazing way to align ourselves with our new goals and dreams, and I want the same for you.

Remember, the universe we live in is made of energy. You are made of energy. The chair you sit on. The bed you sleep in at night. Everything is energy, and all of it is part of our vibrational experience. When you're talking about embracing the next level in your business, you must learn how to use this knowledge to your advantage to make it as easy as possible on yourself. Because you can create anything you desire. But alignment *always* has to come before action.

When you opened this book, you may have been wondering how you can create the next level of success, or the next level in your business and life. Maybe you are struggling to believe you can deal with imposter syndrome, or generally feel that you are not good enough. It is important to acknowledge where you're at, because if we don't know where we're at, we don't know where we are going. If you are currently in a situation that totally sucks, that is totally ok too.

Those "negative" feelings or nudges from inside are very powerful to help you create the next level of success you desire. But how do you embody this new vision you crave? Let me share with you my (not so) *Secrets to Success Formula* to help you embrace your awesomeness and create the success you desire and deserve.

Step 1 - Decide

First of all, you have to decide what you want to achieve. Is it more clients? More impact? Better work-life balance? Hire more staff and have more time off? What is it you want to create for yourself?

Watch out for the shoulds, though. You know, the things you think you should be doing. That's not what I am talking about here. I need you to be honest with yourself and decide what you want (use any "negative" feelings to help you get clear), so you know in what direction you are going. Check your answers from the journaling exercises from the chapters to help you get clarity.

Step 2 - Observe

Step 2 is always a very interesting one. Once you gain clarity about what you want, pay attention to what you start to think. Our minds have a funny habit of wanting to keep us at our current level. Common things to come up are:

- Who am I to want that?
- I could never do that
- I don't know how to make that happen
- This is not the right time
- I can't have both

Write down any negative beliefs that are trying to convince you that you cannot have what you desire. And yes, this may mean you end up with a few pages full of reasons.

Step 3 - Question

When allowing yourself to embody your new level of success, it is important to recognise how helpful your emotions are to guide you towards the new experiences you desire.

Go back to your thoughts from step 2 and ask yourself the following questions:

- Is it ultimately true I cannot have X?
- Is it the highest truth?
- Or could something else also be true?
- What could that be?

So, for example, if you want to cut back on the hours, you work to spend more time with your family. Still, every time you do, something happens in the business that requires your immediate attention. I recommend using these questions to discover any patterns.

What I often see with my clients is that this belief has to do with trust. They don't trust themselves to step back and trust others to keep the business going. So every time they try, something comes up sabotaging their desire to move past this.

Step 4 - Reframe

As you have written out the thoughts and feelings that come to you, and asked yourself these questions, it is time to reframe them in a more powerful, aligned, and empowering way. Lovingly look at the stories you tell yourself and see if you can rewrite the story. Using the example from my coaching business, "cutting back hours to spend time with the family," under step 3, it could be go something like this:

- I want to cut back my hours, but every time I try, it doesn't work.
- Is it ultimately true I cannot have enough time off and run my business? No, because I know people who do manage to do both.
- Is it the highest truth? No, because in this vibrational world, anything is possible.
- Could something else also be true? Yes.
- What could that be? Maybe it would be possible to do things differently, even if I don't know how yet. Maybe I can take Monday morning off to spend with my children this week and see how it goes.

Work through every limiting thought from step 2 and use this process to shift your energy. As you can see from the example, this client shifted from "it wasn't possible" to "it is possible, even though I don't know how yet". This shift allows the universe and the law of attraction to find their way to you, instead of you blocking yourself from it. As you keep working through these, you will discover that in the end, anything is possible if you believe it can be in your reality.

Just keep on going and reframing it until you get to a point where you think and feel: "you know what, I can actually do this!"

Step 5 - Embody

The last, but most certainly not the least important, step is step 5 of this process. As you move through the process and discover how you are keeping yourself from your next level - and start to uncover what could happen for you - it is important to start allowing yourself to feel the new things, desires, or activities to be true. That emotion, that new vibration, is how you embody your next level of success.

Imagine how you would feel knowing you have what it takes to create this next level for yourself. You know you are worthy, you are enough, it is done, and it is on its way to you. How would you feel in this red hot minute if you receive a phone call or a notification on your phone saying that X clients signed up, the money is in your bank account, or the award has been won. How would that feel for you? Start celebrating things now as if it has already happened.

For me, the biggest thing was that I decided I was no longer available for struggle. I'd struggled enough. I'd done my share. And there was no amount of extra struggle I had to do to prove that I was good enough and worthy of my dreams, desires, and goals. I made this decision. I took back my power. I claimed back my birthright to success with ease.

For me, and I see the same with my clients, this is what allowed me to become available for new possibilities. I choose everyday to align myself with things that are fun, easy, and satisfying. Sometimes the contrast knocked me down, but I choose to align myself over and over again with the bigger picture. Because I can create the life I desire. I can have the success I desire and live life on my terms. I am worthy of *anything* I desire. And so are you.

This powerful process works, but it's up to you to start implementing it. Allow yourself a new way of creating, a new way of success (did someone say ease), and a new way of being. However, this process only works if:

- You decide you are worthy
- You decide (and believe) that what you want is possible

I've used my five-step (not so) *Secrets to Success Formula* time and time again. And it shows that real, sustainable long-term success, wellbeing, health, and wealth are possible. The choice is yours.

Embracing Your Awesomeness

"Would you like me to give you a formula for success? It's quite simple, really: Double your rate of failure. You are thinking of failure as the enemy of success. But it isn't at all. You can be discouraged by failure or you can learn from it, so go ahead and make mistakes. Make all you can. Because remember that's where you will find success."

Thomas J. Watson

Once you decide what you want to create, things can shift quickly. Although some goals take a bit longer for the universe to gather the cooperative components, there is no reason why you can't start embodying the success you desire now. As you discovered in the previous chapters, your thought is the first proof of the manifestation of your desire; the feelings are the second; and only the final step is the manifestation of the desire, so you can touch, smell or taste it. If you can feel yourself one with your desire, the universe has to deliver it. It is law.

Sometimes I like to tell myself that I am not *that* special, and that the laws of the universe do not apply to me. I am not that special so marketing doesn't work, or no one cares about me so my dreams can never come true. Even after all the work I've done on myself, my head goes to dark places sometimes. But rather than beating myself up for it, I allow myself to feel it.

If I feel a thought is gaining too much momentum, I talk to my husband or a good friend, who can tell me I am talking nonsense and stop the downward spiral. Sometimes taking a nap is the best thing I can do. Or go for a walk. Or hit a pillow. Don't underestimate the power of these so-called negative moments, because in these lies the contrast; a clear indication of where you *do* want to go. Embrace them, appreciate them, but don't dwell on them.

Before we say goodbye to each other I would like to share with you my final tips on how you can create an outrageously successful life and business by embracing your awesomeness.

First of all, I need you to get crystal clear on your goals by using the journaling exercises in this book.

It is very easy to get stuck in the pattern of just getting things done. But there is a difference between being busy and being productive. Stop and re-evaluate your goals. What would you like to accomplish before the end of the year? Have an epic final sale? Onboard two more clients? Get ready to launch your latest programme? Make sure to set a goal that feels fantastic and start working towards it.

With your goal(s) in mind, you need to come up with a plan that can be easily executed, so I need you to start planning ahead. Break it down into actionable steps. I recommend planning your goals, breaking it down per week, and then into daily activities - from broad to detailed. But remember to plan in time for family, rest and other quality time as well. You don't want to be working during your weekends or family holidays, just to hit your goals. Make time for fun and play too: it is crucial to long-term sustainable health and wealth.

As you align yourself with your new life and the success you are after, it is important to take inspired action. It is very easy to just be busy for the sake of being busy, which in reality is not productive at all. Because there is a difference between being productive and being busy. Just because something is on your to-do list doesn't mean it has to be done.

Learning to prioritise properly is essential to creating the most momentum in your business. I like to think about it this way: what is the number #1 thing I can do today that will have the biggest impact? Think about it in terms of return on investment. Put your energy towards activities that have the biggest return. You will move mountains in no time!

Take time to meditate and listen to those nudges you get from your higher self or intuition. Those little ideas, those sparks - that is where the magic lies. When you follow these inspired ideas - which sometimes can feel like they are way out there - you will have the most magical results.

The next tip is a tricky one, and many struggle with this. So, if this resonates with you, please know you are not alone. Saying no to things that are not in alignment with your goals can feel strange at first. But if you want to focus and get the most out of this year, you've got to focus on what you want to achieve. I know it sounds very logical, but doing this effectively is the one of the biggest stumbling blocks I see my clients struggle with. Let me phrase it differently for you: If it doesn't directly relate to your goal, you've got to say no, or at the very least not now. Most things can wait until next year - if, of course, you want to do it. Just say no and keep repeating; prioritise your to-dos.

For example, as I am writing this book, I could be spending time on the internet, networking and exploring other opportunities. However, as it is my goal to write and publish this book in just twelve weeks, I have to prioritise my time. So if you are not a paying client, my family or my book, you've got to wait until I am done.

And if we are talking about being as aligned and productive as we can be, I need you to value yourself enough (remember you are worthy because you are) to look after yourself properly. You know you perform better when you've had a good night's sleep, eat well, and exercise. More fun, more profits, more joy, more quality time. Right? Make your health and wellbeing your priority. Your future self will thank you for it.

My final tip as you are creating a new reality is that it is important to start looking for evidence that things are working out for you. I know it is very tempting to keep focusing on the things that you don't want, or that are not working. Although these experiences are helpful to help you give birth to new desires, if you only focus on them, the laws of this universe will help you create more of the unwanted.

Look for signs, pennies, feathers, numbers or coincidences, and keep telling yourself you are awesome and it's working. Every positive sign proves things are falling together, and any unwanted sign is just old energy allowing you to appreciate the contrast some more. Remember: no dwelling. But slowly shift your focus to something that feels better and better and better.

Use the power of your consciousness, your power to think and create things into existence, by focusing your energy on what you *do* want. That's where your power lies. The more you do it, the easier it gets. And keep using the guided meditation and other book resources to help you with this.

If shit does hit the fan, it is best just to let it play out. Minimise the damage, get up and try again. Your life is like a story in a book, and just because you are in a painful chapter now, doesn't mean that's how your book will end. And if it is, well, let's just write ourselves a sequel, shall we?

You are amazing. You are so loved and fully supported. You are made of the same stuff that created this whole motherfucking universe and you are so incredibly powerful.

You are enough and you are worthy. And you deserve anything you desire and more.

Remember to keep journaling, keep using the book resources, and listen to the guided meditation daily. And if you want to celebrate your success with me, I would love to hear from you at love@reachsusanne.com. Tag me on social media and remember to add the hashtags #dtmfs or #dropthestruggle. All the links are in the resources.

It was an honour spending this time with you. Here is to you and your success.

Grateful for what is and ready for more,

Susanne

Resources

Book Resources
Download your free book resources at
http://dropthestruggle.co.uk/

Journals
The *Drop The Motherfucking Struggle* Journals
amazon.com/author/susannegrant

Free and Fun Quiz
Uncover your success strategy
grantmethod.com/quiz

Free Masterclass
Your Successful Lifestyle Design Masterclass
grantmethod.com/masterclass

Keynote Speaking & 1:1 Coaching
www.grantmethod.com

About The Author

Susanne Grant is an award-winning Keynote Speaker and Work-Life Balance Integration Expert. She supports CEOs, Entrepreneurs and Conscious Leaders to redefine success in the workplace, so they have the impact they desire without sacrificing their health, relationships or themselves. For themselves, and their teams.

After the birth of her child in 2015, she realised the collective lie "hard work equals success" wasn't working for her and she did not want the next generation to grow up and think this was "normal". So she made a powerful decision. She gave herself permission to break free of the old way of doing business and created a new business model - where holistic health and wealth are an integral part of the business and its success.

Today she runs an award-winning coaching company and hosts sold-out masterminds and events. Her work has been featured in Thrive Global, Authority Magazine, The Global Millionaire Magazine, Billion Success and many other publications. In fact, thousands of people have benefited from her work and are now living life on their terms as they implement Susanne's motto: *"Work Smarter, Not Harder"*.

Website:
http://grantmethod.com/

LinkedIn:
https://www.linkedin.com/in/susannegrant/

Pinterest:
https://www.pinterest.co.uk/susannegrt/

YouTube
https://www.youtube.com/channel/UC8gGphCaZe5HAB gFyKmB9LA

If you enjoyed this book, I would be very grateful if you could leave me a 5-star review, and share your biggest takeaways.

I'd love to celebrate your success with you.

Lightning Source UK Ltd.
Milton Keynes UK
UKHW020653290622
405123UK00009B/575

9 781526 208880